D1518733

ANIMAL ARMIES

DOG PACKS

RICHARD AND LOUISE SPILSBURY

PowerKiDS
press.

New York

Published in 2013 by The Rosen Publishing Group, Inc.
29 East 21st Street, New York, NY 10010

Produced for Rosen by Calcium Creative Ltd
Editors for Calcium Creative Ltd: Sarah Eason and Katie Woolley
US Editor: Sara Antill
Designers: Paul Myerscough and Geoff Ward

Photo credits: Dreamstime: Christian Schmalhofer 18br, Twildlife 16–17; Shutterstock: AISPIX by Image Source 28–29, Mark Atkins 8–9, Kevin Autret 24–25, Bridgena Barnard 6tr, Ewan Chesser 10b, Clearviewstock 12b, Debbie Aird Photography 12–13, Susan Flashman 14–15, Hedrus 22–23, Francois van Heerden 4b, Matt Knoth 8r, Jo McGowan 4–5, Nagel Photography 1, 14tr, 16br, 20–21, 20br, Sean Nel 24br, J Reineke, cover, 10–11, Riekephotos 28r, Richard Seeley 18–19, 22r, Scenic Shutterbug 6–7, Mogens Trolle 26r, Stefanie van der Vinden 26–27.

Library of Congress Cataloging-in-Publication Data

Spilsbury, Richard, 1963–
 Dog packs / by Richard Spilsbury and Louise Spilsbury.
     p. cm. — (Animal armies)
 Includes index.
 ISBN 978-1-4777-0304-5 (library binding) — ISBN 978-1-4777-0330-4 (pbk.) —
ISBN 978-1-4777-0331-1 (6-pack)
1. Wild dogs—Behavior—Juvenile literature. 2. Social behavior in animals—Juvenile literature. I. Spilsbury, Louise. II. Title.
 QL737.C22.S667 2013
 599.77—dc23
                          2012026321

Manufactured in the United States of America

CPSIA Compliance Information: Batch #W13PK2: For Further Information contact Rosen Publishing, New York, New York at 1-800-237-9932

CONTENTS

Wild Dogs 4

Rank 6

On Patrol 8

Hunting 10

Feeding Time 12

New Recruits 14

Training 16

Talking 18

Off Duty 20

Team Building 22

Changes 24

Defending the Pack 26

Survival 28

Glossary 30

Further Reading and Websites 31

Index 32

WILD DOGS

Although wild dogs may look a little like pet dogs, they are wild animals that live in wild places. African wild dogs live in Africa and coyotes live in Canada, the United States, and Mexico. Dingoes live in Australia and wild **dholes** in India. Wild dogs live in many different **habitats**, including **plains**, forests, and mountains.

A group of wild dogs is called a pack. Dingoes and coyotes usually form a pack only to hunt large **prey** together and to have **pups**. A coyote pack is often a family group, made up of parents and their young. African wild dogs and dholes live in groups all the time. There are usually between 5 and 40 dogs in a pack.

African wild dogs are easy to tell apart because each dog has different markings.

African wild dogs live on large plains and in small woodland areas in Africa.

Fight to Survive

Living as a pack means wild dogs trust and understand each other very well. They survive by working together like a well-trained army.

RANK

The members of a human army have different ranks, such as soldiers and leaders. In a dog pack the leaders are the **alpha** male and female. The alpha female is in charge of all the females in the pack, and the alpha male is in charge of all the males. Together the alpha male and female make decisions for the pack, such as when to hunt. The alpha male and female are usually the oldest or biggest of all the dogs in the pack.

African wild dog packs get along very well. Fights like this between pack dogs are very unusual.

Wild dogs in a pack rarely fight each other. Each dog knows its rank, and uses **body language** to show respect to the other dogs. Lower-ranked dogs roll over onto their backs or wag their tails to show they know their place. They even lick the alpha dog's mouth to show they know he is the boss!

Who's Who?

The alpha male and female are the only dogs in the pack that have babies. The other dogs in the pack help the alpha pair to raise and look after their pups.

An alpha male coyote (right) is slightly larger than an alpha female coyote (left).

ON PATROL

Wild dogs have an area called a **territory** in which they live, feed, and sleep. The size of a pack's territory depends on how much food is available. Territories are bigger in areas where there is less food. A pack's territory can be as small as 8 square miles (5 sq km) or as big as 200 square miles (80 sq km). Some African wild dog packs travel across even larger areas.

Wild dogs mark their territory with **urine**. They spray rocks, bushes, and trees as they **patrol** their territory. These scent marks tell other wild dogs to keep out of the pack's territory. The marks also tell other wild dogs to find another place to feed. Some wild dogs, such as coyotes, also use calls to tell other packs where their territory is.

When a wild dog smells a scent mark, it can tell if the territory belongs to a different pack.

*African wild dogs patrol their territory together to keep out **intruders**.*

Who's Who?

Only the alpha pair in an African wild dog pack leaves scent marks. None of the other pack members are allowed to mark the territory.

HUNTING

Wild dogs hunt and eat other animals. By hunting in teams, they can catch large prey such as antelope and deer. Teamwork also helps them to catch prey more often. Coyote packs take turns chasing prey to exhaust the animal. One pair of coyotes chases the prey toward the rest of the pack, then another team takes over the chase, just like a relay! When the prey is exhausted, the pack of coyotes finally catch it.

African wild dogs spread out to chase prey. One team herds it toward another team. This team lies in wait for the prey, sealing off its escape route. Sometimes the dogs attack their prey from different angles, and close in on the animal to bring it down.

African wild dogs rest during the day when it is hot and hunt at dusk or dawn.

African wild dogs have great eyesight and can see prey from far away.

Super Skills

Coyotes are great hunters because they can chase prey quickly. Coyotes can run at speeds of up to 40 miles per hour (65 km/h), which is as fast as a car travels on a main street!

FEEDING TIME

Feeding time is sharing time in a wild dog pack. When prey is caught, all the animals in the pack eat together. If older pups are at an African wild dog kill, they always eat first. The adults eat only once the younger dogs have finished their meal.

Old, sick, or injured adults in the pack cannot help the other dogs hunt. However, the rest of the pack still allows weaker dogs to eat caught prey, and will even carry pieces of meat to them. Sometimes a weaker animal begs a stronger animal to feed it, often by gently pulling at the dog's mouth. The stronger dog then **regurgitates** some of its meal and feeds it to the weaker animal.

Wild dogs eat prey as soon as they have caught it. They eat almost all of the animal.

African wild dogs have large, sharp teeth that can tear through flesh and bite through bone.

Fight to Survive

By hunting as a team, wild dogs capture 8 or 9 prey animals out of every 10 they chase. Most other **predators** catch just 1 in 10 of the prey they hunt!

NEW RECRUITS

An alpha female has pups once a year. Most wild dogs have between 2 and 10 pups in one **litter**, but African wild dogs sometimes have 20. The pups are born in **dens**. These are dark, dry places where the babies are hidden while they are very young. Dens may be a cave or an animal **burrow** no longer in use. For coyotes living near people, the dens may be under sheds, in large drains, or even in holes that the dogs dig in parks!

At first, wild dog pups are small and helpless. They are born blind and their eyes only open after two or three weeks. The mother stays with her pups in the den. Wild dogs are **mammals**, so the pups drink milk from their mother's body. When members of the pack return from a hunting trip, they regurgitate food for the mother.

Although African wild dogs have large litters, few pups survive. They often die from disease or are eaten by lions.

Female dingoes usually have four or five pups in a litter.

Fight to Survive

If another female in a dingo pack has pups, the alpha female kills them. She does this so all of the adult dingoes in the pack will help her to care for her own pups.

TRAINING

Wild dogs start to eat meat from around three weeks old. It is then that the pups' mother starts to hunt once more with the other dogs in the pack. While she is hunting, other members of the pack take turns looking after the pups. When the rest of the pack returns from hunting, the pups beg for food. The dogs then regurgitate it.

When the pups are three months old, the pack usually leaves the den. The pups then begin to follow the adults whenever they go hunting. The pups learn which animals to hunt and where to find them. They learn different **tactics** by watching the adult dogs working as a team.

Wild dog pups soon learn how to work as a team by watching the adults hunt.

Super Skills

Sometimes adults train the pups by catching small prey and then leaving it near the den. The pups then practice their hunting skills by chasing and catching the prey.

Different adults in the pack take turns watching over pups.

TALKING

Wild dogs make different sounds to talk to each other. They squeal, whine, growl, and bark. Wild dogs growl to show anger. They use short barks as alarm calls to warn other pack members that danger is near. African wild dogs also make a call that sounds like a ringing bell. They use this noise to speak to each other over long distances.

Most wild dogs use body language while they hunt, so that they can follow prey silently. The members of a pack wait for the alpha dogs to give the signal that it is time to attack. The leader may do this by pointing its ears toward the prey. African wild dogs also follow the alpha dog's bushy, white-tipped tail. This helps them to stay together while hunting in long grass.

The African wild dog's huge, rounded ears pick up faraway calls from the other members of its pack.

A coyote howls to let other coyotes know where it is and to warn outsiders to stay away.

Super Skills

Dholes do not bark. They whistle instead! Mothers whistle to call their pups, and adults whistle to each other while they hunt. That is why dholes are called the whistling hunters!

OFF DUTY

Wild dogs use a lot of energy chasing prey, so they must rest for much of the day. Coyotes hunt in the night and sleep in the day. African wild dogs hunt in the morning and early evening, so they sleep at night. The pack sleeps together in small groups, with their tails and noses laid across each other.

When they are not hunting or sleeping, African wild dogs spend a lot of time playing and play fighting with each other. Adults and pups play together. They **stalk** and pounce on one another, or chase and wrestle each other in groups. Playing together in this way helps the pack members to **bond** and to feel that they are a team.

African wild dog pups love to jump and play.

African wild dogs rest in the shade during the middle of the day, after their morning hunt.

Fight to Survive

Playing does more than help wild dogs to feel friendly toward each other. It also teaches pups skills such as how to hunt and how to work with the whole pack.

21

TEAM BUILDING

Just like soldiers in an army, wild dogs in a pack depend on each other to survive. They must care for and trust other members of the pack. In an army, soldiers may play sports to build a team that cares about each other. When African wild dogs get together, they use body language to show they care for one another.

One dog runs to another with its mouth open and its ears folded back. The two dogs then rub **muzzles** and gently lick or bite each other's mouths. Then every other dog in the pack joins in. As the dogs get more and more excited, they start to leap at each other and grunt, squeal, and wag their tails.

Coyotes sniff, *nuzzle*, and lick each other to build a caring team.

Super Skills

African wild dogs have a strong smell. When they lick, nuzzle, and rub each other, they share this smell. If a dog is separated from its pack, it finds its way back by following the smell.

African wild dogs bond before they go on a hunt.

CHANGES

Some changes happen to a pack when it faces a problem. Dingoes usually hunt alone, in pairs, or in small family groups. When there is a **drought** the dogs join with other groups to hunt in larger packs. This gives them a better chance of bringing down larger prey and catching more food.

Some changes happen every year. When male coyote pups are nine months old, they leave the pack to form their own group. Females usually stay in the pack. In African wild dog packs, young females leave together when they are around two years old. They join a new pack. Some males may also leave to join a new pack, or form a new pack with a different group of females. However, most stay with their parents' pack.

Young African wild dogs stay together in small packs when they leave their parents' pack.

During a drought, there is little rain and plants die. Animals that eat plants also die, leaving little food for predators such as dingoes.

Fight to Survive

Gangs of young female African wild dogs may have to travel as far as 155 miles (250 km) to join or form a new pack.

DEFENDING THE PACK

Wild dogs have enemies. Wolves and mountain lions catch and eat coyotes. Large wild cats, such as tigers and leopards, kill dholes. Coyotes sometimes fight other coyotes that come near their den when they have young. Wild dogs try to protect themselves and their pack by attacking enemies or predators with their sharp teeth. They often fight to the death.

Lions are feared enemies of the African wild dog. Lions kill pups in dens and attack adult wild dogs. Lions do not usually eat wild dogs. They kill them because the wild dogs hunt the same prey as lions. Sometimes large packs of wild dogs work together to chase off, or even kill, a dangerous lion.

African wild dogs fight enemies such as hyenas.

Fight to Survive

If an African wild dog is injured in a fight, the pack drags it somewhere safe. A pack member takes care of it. It licks any wounds and makes sure the patient gets food when the pack returns from a hunt.

SURVIVAL

People are the biggest threat to wild dog packs. In many areas, people are taking over more and more of the dogs' territory. This means that wild dogs have less land in which to roam and hunt. African wild dog packs need especially large territories. Today they are **endangered** and, unless they are helped, they may die out.

People harm wild dogs in many different ways. Some are killed by accident while crossing highways. Others are killed by farmers who believe that wild dogs kill their farm animals. Some people shoot coyotes because they fear the wild dogs will attack them or their pets. However, coyotes that live near towns may actually help people by killing pests that spread disease, such as rats.

Some wild dogs are killed by cars on highways that cut through the dogs' territories.

Some African wild dog packs live safely in African national parks.

Fight to Survive

People are helping to protect wild dogs, such as dholes and African wild dogs, by creating **reserves** and national parks. These are areas of land where people cannot build and where the wild dogs can live safely.

29

GLOSSARY

alpha (AL-fuh) An animal with the highest rank in a group, the leader of the group.

body language (BAH-dee LANG-gwij) Actions animal use to talk.

bond (BOND) To feel close to another animal.

burrow (BUR-oh) The hole an animal lives in underground.

dens (DENZ) Places in which wild dogs have their babies.

dholes (DOHLZ) Fierce wild dogs that live in Southeast Asia.

drought (DROWT) A long time with little or no rain.

endangered (in-DAYN-jerd) When an animal could die out.

habitats (HA-buh-tatz) Places in which animals hunt and live.

intruders (in-TROOD-erz) People or animals that are unwelcome

litter (LIH-ter) The babies that an animal has at one time.

mammals (MA-mulz) Animals that give birth to live young.

muzzles (MUH-zelz) Areas around dogs' mouths.

nuzzle (NUH-zel) To rub against, to show affection.

patrol (puh-TROHL) To move around an area to make sure it is safe.

plains (PLAYNZ) Large areas of flat land with few trees.

predators (PREH-duh-terz) Animals that hunt other animals.

prey (PRAY) An animal that is eaten by other animals.

pups (PUPS) Baby dogs.

regurgitates (ree-GUR-juh-taytz) Brings swallowed food up again.

reserves (rih-ZURVZ) Areas of land where animals are protected.

stalk (STOK) To follow prey quietly before attacking it.

tactics (TAK-tiks) Tricks or ways of doing something.

territory (TER-uh-tor-ee) An area controlled by one animal group.

urine (YUR-un) A liquid waste made by the body.

FURTHER READING

Quinlan, Julia J. *Dingoes*. Ferocious Fighting Animals.
   New York: PowerKids Press, 2013.

Murdoch, J. D., and M. S. Becker. *The African Wild Dog*.
   The Library of Wolves and Wild Dogs. New York:
   PowerKids Press, 2002.

Vogel, Julia. *Coyotes*. Our Wild World. Lanham, MD:
   Cooper Square Publishing, 2008.

WEBSITES

Due to the changing nature of Internet links, PowerKids Press has developed an online list of websites related to the subject of this book. This site is updated regularly. Please use this link to access the list:
www.powerkidslinks.com/aarmy/dog/

INDEX

A
African wild dogs, 4, 8–10, 12,
    14, 16, 18, 20, 22–29
alpha females, 6–7, 9,
    14–15, 18
alpha males, 6–7, 9, 18

B
body language, 6, 18, 22

C
coyotes, 4, 8, 10–11, 14, 20,
    24, 26, 28

D
dens, 14, 16–17, 26
dholes, 4, 19, 26, 29
dingoes, 4, 15, 24

F
fighting, 6, 20, 26–27
food and hunting, 4, 6, 8,
    10–14, 16–17, 18–21, 24,
    26–27

L
learning and training, 16–17
lions, 26

N
national parks, 29

P
people, 14, 28–29
playing, 20–22
predators, 13, 26
prey, 4, 10–13, 17–18, 20,
    24, 26
pups, 4, 7, 12, 14–17, 19–21,
    24, 26

R
reserves, 29

S
scent marks, 8–9
sleep, 8, 20
sounds, 18–19

T
territories, 8–9, 28